W9-CQM-283

NORTHERN EXPOSURES

NORTHERN EXPOSURES

PHOTOGRAPHS BY
ROB MORROW

HYPERION

NEW YORK

Book design by Holly McNeely

Library of Congress Cataloging-in-Publication Data
Morrow, Rob.
Northern exposures : photographs / by Rob Morrow.
p. cm.
ISBN 0-7868-6064-2
1. Northern exposures (Television program)   I. Title.
PN1992.77.N67M67 1994
791.45'72—dc20
94-6299
CIP

First Edition
10 9 8 7 6 5 4 3 2 1

SPECIAL THANKS TO

Everyone at Northern Exposure
Dan Strone
Scott Zimmerman
Craig Nelson
Ivey Seright
Tokyo Photo
Frank Prinzi, Jim Haymen, and Gordon Lonsdale
for allowing me to capture their light
and
especially my dedicated assistant
Corrine Luesing

Most actors, even the ones fortunate enough to make a living, find themselves with a fair amount of downtime (time they are not working). Before *Northern Exposure* I certainly had my share. I realized pretty early that there were two things I could do: one, tending toward the self-destructive; the other, more constructive. I opted for the latter and studied photography at the New School in New York City. I built a darkroom in my apartment and entered the fascinating world of developing and printing. This went on for a good many years, taking many photographs and making many prints. I would give them as gifts after shows that I'd worked on or trips I'd taken with people. I developed a habit of carrying a camera with me pretty much wherever I went, and this carried over to my time on *Northern Exposure*. After a few years I realized that I had accumulated a couple hundred photographs of the lives of people making our show. These were basically for my own personal album, but I would give gifts of the photographs I liked to the people who were in them. What struck me about the images was the difference between what a still person might have captured and what I did. Because of the intimacy that I share with a lot of the people in the pictures I was allowed access that other photographers would not necessarily be given. Actors can tighten when a still person is on the set, but they let their guard down around me because they know me. As a result I think I was able to capture some moments of truth. After looking at the accumulation of these photos it occurred to me that other people, fans of the show, might be interested in looking at them as well. I hope you enjoy looking at them as much as I enjoyed taking them. I am grateful to have spent time with the people in these pictures.

NORTHERN EXPOSURES

I always find something surreal
about an exterior night location.
It's like trying to bend nature to
our own needs.

While Cicely may be in Alaska, Roselyn (where we shoot the show) is in the Cascades of Washington. Unfortunately, we do not get near the amount of snowfall as they do in Cicely. These are styrofoam snowdrifts being moved into place to create our illusion.

Like Cicely,
Roselyn has its
own bunch of
wonderful
characters.

Some of us take photos between scenes, some of us practice
our roping. Here, Barry Corbin at one of his hobbies.

Some read: John Cullum.

Some write letters: Becky Revak,
of our sound department.

Scout, who can be seen running
about in many a scene on the show,
is here assisting George San Pietro,
our dolly grip, as he balances the
camera tracks.

The cast ready and waiting...and waiting...and waiting.

John Corbett had particular fun with this episode. His character Chris had created a contraption known as "the Fling." This would-be performance art piece catapults an inanimate object into the air to its eventual destruction, just for the sake of doing it. In this case it was a piano. The Dadaists would have loved Chris.

John has a most mercurial face. Here he is looking nothing like the normal Holling,

This to me clearly captures the difference between Darren Burrows and his character Ed.

Bill Irwin is an occasional guest on the show. His true talent has yet to be captured on film and I strongly urge anyone to go see his live performances. He is a very special performer.

TOP LEFT: Janine is never withholding of a kiss or a hug and John doesn't seem to mind.

LEFT: Although Tim Whidbee is our set dresser, he has the spirit of a Zen guru. He is always there with some clever and insightful observation.

This balloon was from a sequence for a Thanksgiving episode. The Native Americans in Cicely co-opt the Mexican Day of the Dead tradition to celebrate. Woody Crocker, our set designer, never ceases to amaze me and to top himself. He cannot be given too much credit. One has the sense that if he were asked on Tuesday night to construct a set of the Sistine Chapel, it would be ready Wednesday morning.

(OPPOSITE) Darren in his Day of the Dead regalia.

Focus puller and camera operator Greg Collier.

(OPPOSITE, TOP) Bob Loeser, our second-assistant director, had his hands full on this episode directing the many extras.

(OPPOSITE, BOTTOM) The nice thing about being a regular on the series is that you get visited by all kinds of wonderful actors as guest stars. I really enjoyed having Tony Edwards around. It also breaks up the monotony of working with the same people day in and day out.

The character
of Chris is such
an original.
Great costume.

Rob Thompson, one of our executive producers and directors, guides John.

Catherine Bentley, our costume designer, pursues her tasks with a childlike joy. Here she is flanked by her team, Nina Moser and Marilee Melgaard.

Doing twenty-two shows a year can sometimes get monotonous. Fortunately every once in a while the writers will offer a new challenge. We all enjoyed the "Cicely Show," when we went back to the founding days of Cicely at the turn of the century. Emmy Award–winning Frank Prinzi, our director of photography, had a field day creating the era.

I believe Cynthia Geary and Darren Burrows are the two least like their characters on the show. Here Cynthia's cognizant gaze has not a trace of Shelly.

Darren,
as Ed's alter ego
turn-of-the-century
self, recites poetry
in the Cicely
episode.

John and Barry relished the idea of playing the "bad guys" in the Cicely episode.

(LEFT) Patrick Phillips, a set dresser, is one of those responsible for all of the wonderful attention to detail you see on our sets.

Quite often, as in our Cicely episode, different kinds of smoke are used to diffuse light. It looks great but wreaks havoc on one's respiratory system. Imagine being at a party where every single person smoked but you. Here Janine copes between takes with a gas mask.

(OPPOSITE) Executive producer and director Michael Fresco directs Tony and Janine in a scene.

The wonderfully imaginative performance group Mummenschanz came through town with Bill Irwin in an episode. They were really fun and I recommend catching their show if it's ever around.

(OPPOSITE) Janine Turner with prop master Dick Kyker.

It was a real honor having David Hemmings on the show. Film aficionados will remember him from the Antonioni film *Blow Up*.

This was a dream sequence of Ed's where he imagined Cicely in a kind of post-apocalyptic nightmare. Again it afforded Frank Prinzi the opportunity to have some fun with the lighting.

John with his own
air source.

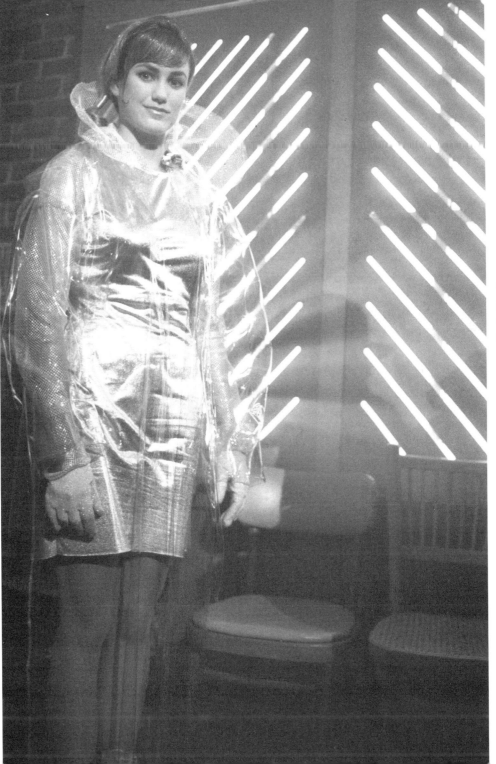

Cynthia in her
post-apocalyptic
environmentally
protective dress.

Life goes on—John between takes.

(OPPOSITE, LEFT) Duncan Sobel, an electrician, is perched on a catwalk, focusing a light. Someone has to do it.
(OPPOSITE, RIGHT) Dean Parisot, seen here with John, is one of our frequent guest directors. I find him really talented and I always look forward to working with him. He won an Academy Award for a beautiful short film *The Appointments of Dennis Jennings*, starring and co-written by Steven Wright. If you ever get a chance to catch it, don't miss it.
(BELOW) Paul Vollo, a.k.a. Paulie, is a grip. Here he's making sure everything is okay.

Janine.
(OPPOSITE, LEFT) Janine, via make-up person Denise Della Valle, makes sure
there is nothing in her teeth after dinner.
(OPPOSITE, RIGHT) This was Janine's post-apocalyptic look. It was not easy to get
her to let me take this photo, but with a face like hers, I can understand.

Grip Ryan Purcell doesn't seem to mind the cold too much.

Lisa McCullough is Janine's stunt double—she also doubled her in the movie *Cliffhanger*.

Peter Bradshaw and Tim Widbee. Peter is my stand-in.
(OPPOSITE) Even though we do not get the snow we always want, it certainly can be brutally cold.
Patrick is bundled against the elements.

Jim Charleston is one of our first-assistant directors and directed some very nice episodes as well.

(LEFT) Camera operator Dave Frederick wearing the same parka that I wear on the show. It is said to be good to -70°. I would like to know whom they tested to find out.

(OPPOSITE) Not only are you going to stand outside at -5° for hours on end but giant fans are going to turn on you to make it look windy. Glamorous, huh? This is called a Ritter fan and that is Patrick once again.

I don't think Barry was looking forward to standing out in the cold this day.

Janine.

Director of photography Frank Prinzi. (OPPOSITE) Frank oversees his lighting.

John checks
his hair.

John, who has a very puckish spirit, is always willing to play around for me when I pull out the camera.

Richard Cumings, seen here with Tim, plays Bernard who is Chris's brother. It is my favorite story line of all the story lines.

John and Richard.

John and Cynthia.

John.

Scott Paulin was a guest star. He played the only homeless person ever in Cicely.

This picture fails to show the true uniqueness of this set. It was one of Chris's many performance art pieces. He had gone about the town collecting different kinds of light sources and created this sculpture. It was really spectacular to see.

Peg Phillips and Darren.

Elaine Miles. Since she was not an actress when she started the show, I am amazed at how much I've learned working with her. I truly adore her.

Mary Loibl is an assistant to the producers and a big fan of Beverly Hills 90210.

Gaffer Scott Williams and script supervisor Barbara "Babs" Brown.

Our caterers, Rob Gray, Bob Eaton, and Sandra Doyle, are some of the best in the biz.

These gargoyles were made for a Shakespearean dream sequence of Maurice's that never aired. It is amazing the amount of work done in films that never makes it to a final cut. This is Marne Cohen, paint shop foreman.

Catherine Dixon, art department.

John had to be muddy in this scene and he had the choice of going to make-up or doing it himself.

John and Janine.

I guess Darren got sick of me taking his picture.

Jim Charleston, our beloved first-assistant director. This was his first day as a director.

I always thought Janine looks a bit like Elizabeth Taylor in these shots.

The
great
face of
Peg.

Casting assistant
Marie Rose
Ponath makes
her extra debut
as a
mosquito.

Grand Dame Peg,
between shots.

Peg.

There was an episode where Ben and Jerry's ice cream was mentioned. To show appreciation, when Ben and Jerry were passing through town, they stopped by the set and served up some of their dreamy concoctions. This is Ben.

Wardrobe assistant Sandra Bush and costume supervisor Marilee Melgaard.

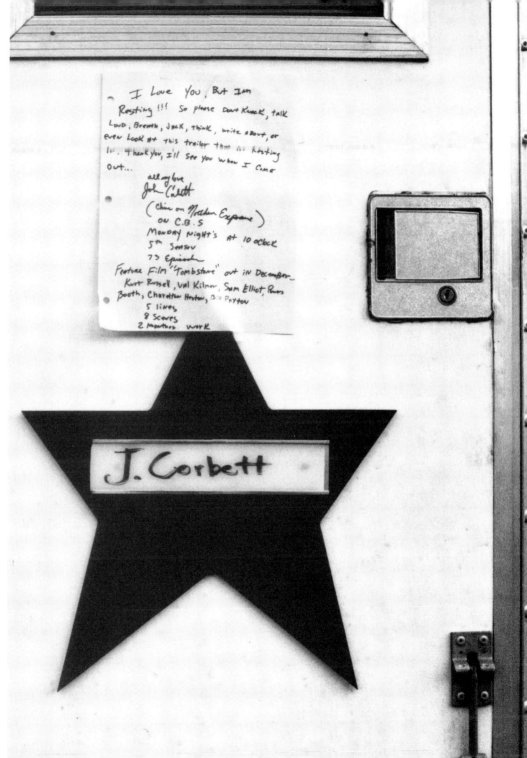

The door to John Corbett's trailer.
(OPPOSITE, TOP) Marilee Melgaard, costume supervisor, and Sandra Bush, wardrobe assistant. Every moment's a blast. (OPPOSITE, BOTTOM) Tim and Patrick.

Janine with our much loved guest star Valerie Mahaphee, who plays Eve. I have a hard time keeping a straight face when I work with her.

Elaine and Lori Smith,
an extra.

Adam Arkin is like a brother to me—there is something in each of us that makes the other laugh. When we first started working together, we could add two hours to the workday because of laughing. It is always fun when he is around.

Yours truly.